dance of the day

Sanuli Karunaratne's poems are a warm, intimate voice whispering you image-deep secrets in a sensory voice. A poet to watch.

—**Karen Comer**
writer and judge of the Dorethea Mackellar Poetry Award, 2024

dance of the day

a short collection of poems

sanuli karunaratne

to ammi, thaththi, and aiyya i'm forever grateful

Copyright text and line art © Sanuli Karunaratne 2025

ISBN 978-1-7641032-9-9

All rights reserved.
Without limiting the rights under copyright above,
no part of this publication may be reproduced,
stored in or introduced into a retrieval system,
or transmitted in any form or by any means
(electronic, mechanical, photocopying, recording
or otherwise), without the prior written permission
of the author.

No AI Training: Without in any way limiting the author's
[and publisher's] exclusive rights under copyright,
any use of this publication to "train" generative artificial
intelligence (AI) technologies to generate text is expressly prohibited.
The author reserves all rights to license uses of this work for
generative AI training and development of machine learning
language models.

Published by
Forty South Publishing Pty Ltd, Hobart, Tasmania
fortysouth.com.au

Printed by IngramSpark

contents

sun's blessings *1*
dance of the day *2*
paths and other uninteresting things *3*
where reality can't reach us *5*
fingers through my hair *7*
sprite, stars, and salt *9*
swinging on the swing set *11*
summer *12*
autumn *14*
stage directions *15*
the unseen *16*
under leaves *18*
forest's memories *20*
sink into the deep *22*
the convergence *23*
maybe i was the one who left *25*
quiet evenings *27*
a getaway trip *28*
i have an idea *29*
the adjudicator *32*
sempiternal *34*
open eyes at night *36*
whales and rose petals (in your dreams) *38*
the antonym *40*
all or nothing *42*
what never leaves *44*
stolen *46*

about the author *49*

sun's blessings

the sun gives me her bones
(pure ivory mixed with the
hardened flesh of honeycomb)
in the letters of sparkling
golden nectar she sends me,
filling me like a mug of
something warm and sweet –

every morning, she leaves
for me: a clipping of her
ethereal hair, dark golden
like burnt caramel and sugar,
or the bark of a deep, settled
maple tree – and every evening,
before she leaves with a
glint of a simple smile,

she whispers a breathy truth
into the ridges of my ear,
and bids me goodbye, the
smell of burning light and
honey painting the sky with
kissed pink, dripping like oil.

dance of the day

they intertwine, a glorious melody
full of breathless, timeless laughter
the breeze dances in the air
the tang of the grassy spring scent

flows on the freshly emerging leaves
white daisies dot the evergreen fields
like stars in the darkness of the night
but now is not the time to dwell on the dark –

now is the light, only the light to guide us
and we thrive in the sun-kissed valleys
we run in the blur of the sweeping wind
crushing daisies beneath our feet,

our bodies draped in the joyous hands of love
and we live millennia in a stuttering heartbeat
for we bend time with the edges of our smiles
the clouds watch us, as we watch them –

they change with the shades of the sky above
from the morning gold to the midday blue –
but the sleep of night is long forgotten,
it has no place in the lightness of the day,

where there are no inky shadows spilling over
for the monsters and the nightmares to lie in wait
here, in the daytime, there is no fear –
only pure, unbridled joy.

paths and other uninteresting things

there is a path there, lain amongst
the bushes, where the nails of the
ground lay outstretched against the
sky. there is a path there, to dance
with, to feel the swift brush of
feather-light ferns, and see the
watery embrace of moss on
rock.

on this path, i go, with the tapestry
of your back pasted onto my eyes,
as the grass shivers for my attention,
and tall bark stands proud and
awaiting – but only you catch my eye,
again and again and
again.

there is a path here, for wandering
souls, but i am a soul that has wandered
and has pondered, but still cannot
find meaning in anything that isn't
you.

... /

there is a path here, where the
creatures care more about moonlight
than they care about anything to do
with the sun, but you, wonderful
cloud-eyed you, you make them
care.

and i would much rather bask
in the glory of your nails, warm
and precise, your hair, true and
long and earth-swept, and your full,
heart-peeling embrace

than anything
else this path would ever have to
offer.

where reality can't reach us

the chuckle of a ditzy stream,
meandering past the frivolous
grass, dripping with green light
and honey. the sun is an eye
into the supernatural, into what
lies beyond blue skies and yellow
dots of daffodils, and its knowing
gaze feels eerie on tanned skin.

naturally, accompanied by all
of these beautiful colours, there
is laughter; playful, effortless,
sinking into seas of warm grass
and far-away quietness. and there,
you can find me, with a glass
of strawberry lemonade and a
well-loved book in the welcome
arms of a dear friend.

we exchange meaningless (and
somehow poetic) thoughts, things
like how cheesecake tastes like the
moon's lips, things like how the
wonderful fizz of lemonade settles
nicely in your cheeks, things like
how, when you smile, it reminds me
of a small pearl lying on a sandy beach.

... /

have you guessed what i'm describing
yet? this is, to me, what i dream of at
night, when the curtains are drawn
and the door is shut, and reality is busy
making someone else's life a misery.
this is what i want the rest of my life
to be, endless and sunny with a
promise of clear, wide skies, all tied
up into a nice and neat romance.

fingers through my hair

lying on the back of a story,
knee-deep in a hot soup of
caramel sunlight, eyes closed
to a backdrop of secrets that exist
in the crackly smoothness of
only voices. she parts through
dark waves with ease, like the
tide obeys the moon's grasp.

fingers raking through hair –
except it is much bigger,
much closer, it is the opposite
of drowning – floating in the big,
over-encompassing feeling
that spans the length of my
mother's fingertips, and the
summers of seven million years.

a long, long time ago, when
feelings were yet to be named
 and poetry was yet to be touched,
there was a tree, big and blooming
and tough, and in the tree was
me, and my mother, and my great –
great-grandmother, and all of
their great-grandmothers,
and they are running fingers
through each other's hair.

... /

and there, they are laying the rocks
of a story that will become a
pond will become a lake,
will become the ocean of my blood,
and i close my eyes to see the
secrets, and my mother runs her
fingers – with her seven million –
year-old-skin – through my hair,
and there is nothing but
the sound of light.

sprite, stars, and salt

there is a multiverse of people,
all inside of me, inside the closed
possibilities of my flesh. they
tangle and thread into each
other, a blurry phantom of
melded memories and views.

they whisper through the hairs
on my arms, through the nails
on my fingers. they are a current
of rising tides, frothy and mixed
and screaming white. they sing
through me. my voice cracks
in their name.

my childhood friend taught me
how to draw stars in the random
sand of a road, and now they litter
the backs of my test papers. once,
my stomach touched the bottom
of oceans, and my eyes their salt,
sharing iced popsicles with two
girls whom i was yet to truly know.

... /

sometimes i look at a bottle of
sprite and think about how my brother
always used to choose it at the
movie theatre, but he doesn't
like its taste anymore.

i think about the stars in the sand,
and i think about how they repaved
that road a few years ago. i think about
the water against my stomach, and
realise i don't remember where
exactly we were. i think about how
every time i go to a movie theatre
i choose sprite but my brother
chooses pepsi and think,

you have moved on without me.

so many dead memories, dead
roads, dead oceans. and they're
all in me. through test papers,
salt, and movie theatre sprite.

swinging on the swing set

the wind whistles, a blanket of ruffling sound
over the squinting grey of the playground, the
groan of trees and evergreen ferns.
the creak of the swing-set trills in harmony, up
and   down   and   back up again.
in this husk of the neighbourhood, this avenue
of glistening and groaning grey, no one steps
on the grass. the flying fox remains in its age-old
peace, screeching with hostility when the wind
coerces it forward.
the grip of the swings feels cold and unforgiving
on young hands, on newly wrinkled palms. yet
the swing hums thoughtfully, a pondering tune.
the eyes of brick houses peer curiously, as do
the melting clouds high up in the sky. a wash of
deep, dire dark swims over the playground, a
cloth of ice and gloom. the swing-set keeps on,
up and   down   and   back up again.
but then, when young palms are bruised with
silver sting and smothered in growling grey, the
sun parts the clouds with pale, piercing fingertips,
and all throughout the blinding blue of the
playground, the laugh of trees and evergreen ferns
can be heard.

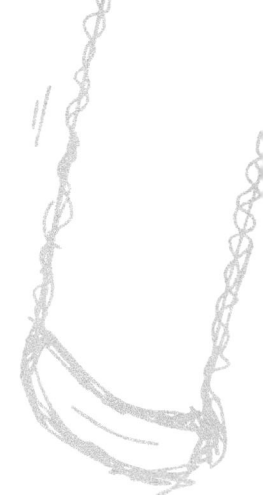

summer

the sun bakes away the sadness of winter,
evaporating like daydreams in summer –
here, everything is blindingly bright, a
reality that i am not used to – the wet green
of the trees sways in relief and familiarity
they are used to this unrelenting warmth,
whereas i am the frost of the colder months,
melting under the lulling tint of the sunlight

the breeze is sickeningly sweet, carrying
the dreams of bees and the longings of flowers,
and i feel eternally content, filled to the
brim with the rays of the sun, who owns
this court of blossoming blooms and
glimmering lakes of clear, syrupy water –
it is cool to the touch, but sends a shiver
of startling comfort down to the very depths of
this shadow i call my soul –

the water coaxes it out of the chasm
deep inside me, teasing it with flickering
morsels of happiness – and like a moth to
a flame, but instead a butterfly to a glorious
sun, it follows a being old and true, of
the dreams of bees and the longings of
flowers, and what my soul finds is not
happiness, but something even truer than
the suffering that lines this canvas of a world –

deep within me, and lukewarm around me,
i find the seed of the world, laid bare and
brittle, baking in the sunlight that i, myself,
am – weathered by what it has borne, eroded
by what it has become – and among the dreams
of bees, and the longings of flowers, i find
the reality of reality.

autumn

sometime between the yawns of the morning and the snores
of the night, it has rained, and it dyes my shoes a glossy, happy,
black. the grass scratches against my legs, and it peels away
the skin that grew under warm bedsheets. my hair is in tufts,
obeying the whim of the whimsical winds, and if my skin
had not known the voice of the sun, it would be blushing with
the cold fever of autumn.

sometime between the beats of my heart and the distance between
our fingers, something has changed, irrevocably, unchangeably,
irreversibly. there is a bird in the sky, so far into the Blue, into
that which swirls and dances at dusk, and i watch it fly by with
a joy that sinks deep into my nerves, that strokes the cells of my
blood. it fizzes like sunlight on a pond, and then it drifts.

oh, how it drifts.

so that's how it goes: light and love and grey in autumn. in autumn,
there are clouds, and down below,
far,
far below, there is me,
with my hands outstretched, with the wind in my hair and the grass against
my legs, and the dew in my shoes, and the birds, they fly up above,
up with the clouds, and i am shining like sunlight on a pond.

stage directions

Roses: threaded into a wreath of red and romance, Fingers: sewing idly, languid, distracted. Neck: opened to the viewer, splayed on display by the passionate and evocative hands of the Sun: *look? can't you see? how i chase the shadows away?*

Eyes: spun around and around on a spool of curiosity, hidden by perspective. Hair: cascaded down beneath the shoulders, auburn awned to the nines. You: off-balance, out of orbit, floating in random precision. Her: tethered to the hotel room floor, condensed into scenery, here Forever.

Regret: stuck between the eyes, above the nose, where annoyance is optimal, embroidered into the stage props. Heart: attached to you by obligation, donated, pending approval (hers). Mind: clouded, foaming, slippery like the waves she watches before windows.

Roses: complete, ended, released from the ornery of verbs. Fingers: reddened, sore, drizzled and buttered in sweet, salty blood. Neck: opened to the viewer, though the shade is trickling in scarily quick, sliding into zero, permitted by the Sun: *look. i'm sorry, but your time is up. Forever ends in approximately 4.3 milliseconds.*

the unseen

you can see it, see it everywhere –
see it in the way the boy skids
around on the court, fluid in the
way the foam at the bottom of
a waterfall slides over smooth
pebbles, bubbly and violent;

see it in the hazy mumbles of the
girl scribbling messy equations into
her book, hand moving furiously
across the page, biting her lip in
practiced concentration;

see it in the way
the child glides across the water,
sleek water peeling off of his
tanned skin in ripples of coolness;
see it in the second before the
woman finishes thumbing the keys
of her piano in a soft solo;

in the coarse breath before toned
legs leap expertly off the diving
board, down, down, into sweltering
blue – see it, see it in every glimmer
of subtle personality, see all that is
not seen –

notice the presence of talent and
see experience, glance at the
vision of perfection and see tears
on the pages of exam booklets,
look at blended brushstrokes crafted
by chance and see hundreds of
carefully plotted first drafts –

see it all, the passion, the
the learning – see all that is not seen.

under leaves

she stays, like a bird, under the rain, shielded by the long, outstretched arms of leaves. the moments pass like flower petals in spring – they give her a quick, dismissing glance, and then they are gone.

the rain comes, with the quiet discrepancy of summer, and some of it finds its way through the viridian veins, but most is a distant thud, a cool battering above. it does not affect her – at least, not enough to topple her from her spot squeezed against the bark – and so she stays there: silent, still, siphoned off from the steady stream of time.

occasionally, the sun leaks through the leaves in jagged strokes, blinding her with meaningless things, like hope and promises and the future, but then she blinks – and it vanishes with the mercy of her eyelashes. the sun relents and retreats back into the sea. some days, though, it stays till the moon drags it away, and some days, when the blood beneath her flesh runs cold, it leaves with the clouds. but it never stays long enough to make her believe.

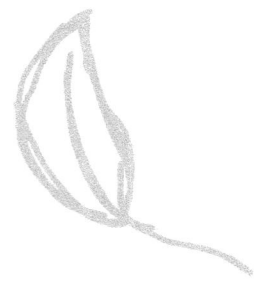

the leaves block her view, and she is thankful. whatever
is out there, whether it makes her sob or laugh or stare,
she knows it's not worth it. it never has been. so, she is
thankful, to the leaves, who shield her from the trickery
and the lies. she is thankful to her tapered blindfolds,
who let her see it all from the outside, where the sun can
never shine bright enough to seduce her. her life does
not exist, not here, where she is everything that she
could never be when the sun could see her face.
and so, she stays: the bark etches tattoos onto her back,
and the beetles and the bugs never scare her. everything
is temporary, all gone in a splash of light, stolen in a streak
of darkness.
everything, except her: under the leaves, head tilted towards
a reflection of the sun, eyes closed to the rest of the world.
she is immortal: nothing can hurt her, nothing can love her,
nothing can touch her. and in a world where love and hate
both exist in tandem, where they are on the same side of a
one-dimensional coin, she exists outside. untouchable. safe.

to her, what matters is the rustling of leaves, and the grating
touch of bark, and nothing else
exists.

forest's memories

how many lives have been
lived in this forest of evergreens?
have my ancestors filled its
cold, full air with stories and
tales around a flickering campfire,
speaking in a language
remembered only by the oldest
trees, embedded in their gnarled
bark like frozen sap –

how many have lived lives full
of wonder and imagination, had
their fill of listening to the echoing
call of the void, and painted their
dreams with its voice? how many,
tell me, were poets; their children
passing down their words through
the bone and muscle of their mouths –

how many were artists; fingerpainting
the edges of spears and the flesh of
bulls on their cave walls? how many
were the architects, the actors, the
playwrights – how many of them thought
and observed and wept over our world,
long before the trees learnt the harsh
edges of our words? this forest that i
walk through carries the names and the
loves and the words of our ancestors –

the poets, the artists, and the playwrights,
all who shaped this muddy ground with
the thud of the soles of their feet – how many,
i ask you, because i know they were here,
and i know how they thought and observed
and wept over this world – this world that
we are turning to dust.

sink into the deep

deep, deep, deep –
the water churns around me,
a dazzling whirlpool cracked
into fractals of reflected sunlight,
as my brain bobs about in my
head like a buoy lost at sea –

the drifting waves pass over me
like sheets of laundry, cool and
gentle, sinking beneath my flesh,
devolving into schools of sleek,
glimmering fish deep in my bloodstream

my breath goes stale in the
comfort of my lungs, a tiny
moment of time locked in an
air-tight container – my hair
is a reef of dark, swimming

worms, slithering amongst the
waves in families, and they
sting against my fluttering eyelashes,
jellyfish of their own accord,
as i sink, sink, sink.

the convergence

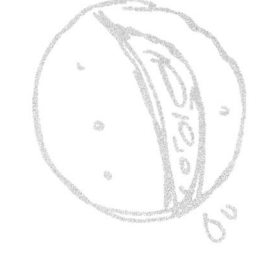

there is a point
when

the archaic, thick, morose dust of home, of betrayal, of change, the warm milk of childhood, offered in the remnants of clay and well-loved ceramics, the feeling of water in a stream tracing the veins of sticky blood, the aggression of a ripe mandarin – the spurt of cold juice against teeth, the ceremonial heaviness of adulthood on the crown of one's sorrowful head, the simplicity of play, the melding of imagination and freedom into fulfilment, into life

meets

the urban shock of the traffic, of the throngs of sweaty, strange people, red lights in rain, the commercial delivery of a new package every other Thursday, the crinkly, crawling sound of plastic and cling wrap, the ominous gaps of light in the night sky where there should be the pale, quiet, darkness, the endless, clawing urge to seek entertainment, to laugh, to cry, the emptiness of the self, the inability to drink from the pond of the soul

there, where

humanity sinks into the murmuring, into the echo chamber of voices, where every soulless, mindless thought is broadcast unnaturally, artificially, where the powers that be are all against the reality of human nature –

... /

where home is the gap between houses, where milk is no longer rooted in humility, where it forms in the satirical sanctity of plastic cup after plastic cup, where the streams have dried up, have dissolved into black oil, where the showerhead is the waterfall, where the fruit is condensed is processed is squeezed into 100% Sugar-Free Orange Juice! :)

and the teeth are too busy facing the snow-white of acid, where adulthood is a curse, and wrinkles can be stretched into oblivion, where play is the endless click, the downward scroll, the melding of solitude and entertainment into loneliness, into

life?

maybe i was the one who left

i made a promise to myself, long before
the sky dripped into ashen day, when the
ocean did not long for me from
windows.
the rock was still new, i swore it! it was a
million, but then
none,
it smelled fresh, a wandering whiff of revival.
the grass grew deeper, wrestled with the
not-yet sweat of the soil. ancestor of the
jack-jumper, seven thousand kilometres
before, when it littered my feet with its legacy.

this world will still be here,
is what was
said.
not through mouth, not with tongue,
but in my laidback absorbance of it all.
the well of contentment that slopped and
slipped inside me. the way i thought
nothing of the traffic outside, the
lopsided bellowing
of the trucks and
vans. the way i traced the coarseness
of the walls, blinked at the fluorescent
paint.

... /

i promised myself, a little spool of thready innocence
right here where my brain should be.
and when my skin grew wild like vines over fingers, when it
burst into brown and tan and sun-child over my face,
the thread,
the promise
it stayed there. unfurled slowly, grew to know grey
skies and unfamiliar winds, sobbed when the air
became devoid of the sound of motors and horns.
time split into the tiniest of fibres, tines of a forlorn fork,
and they stretched and stretched until the shock
was like a big black garbage bag.

i had outlived everyone,
everything.
i had loved
enough to watch the rock grow cracks and
gather dust, ivory ichor, lava expanding,
moss flourishing. i wait, a quiet noise,
as the jack-jumpers burrow into soils
dehydrated. i wear shoes now.
the world will still be here,
was the promise. it was only
seven thousand kilometres
after that i learnt it was not mine to
break.

quiet evenings

the crooning of the birds
emphasises the warmth of
the muted blaze of the
fireplace numbing the cold
with stolen heat and
the burning scent of cherry

hushed whispers and secrets,
the knocking of the swaying
trees against the glass window,
the worn-out arm of the
weary sofa nestled under
the weight of our knees

long forgotten jasmine tea
and burnt-out lavender
scented candles, sweeping
smoke of shaded fields
of sleepy violet and vanilla,
faces hidden behind
cold-shaped fingers and
palms

soft cradling laughter and
unnecessary
secrets and truths sing
the melody of a lifetime
of quiet evenings, the
chorus humming us
melting lullabies.

a getaway trip

the trees feel utterly vacant in their flapping,
in their slow, incessant wave with the wind,
in and out, merging with the sounds of air
and birds.
the grass is almost floating in the dredges of
wet mud and water, and it spills all over socks
and shoes like tears. for the traveller, who
strides across
the forest, every sensation is dunked in the cold,
toxic venom of winter, coated in ice and
indifference, slowed into a chittering halt by the
empty howling of
the storm clouds.
like the forest, entrenched in ice and the stuff
of loneliness, so is the mind of the traveller.
whilst the ears hear the sweep of birds' wings
and the mouth tastes the frigidity of the
mountain air
it stays, stubbornly frozen in place, still in the
isolation and keening, the suffocating warmth of
home.
when the mist clears, and the bones ache and
whisper of fatigue, he shall find himself in the
same warmth he ran to escape, and no more of
his loneliness
is less than what it was when he left.
the cold outside was never a match for the innate
stagnancy of his being.

I have an idea

i shiver in between the margins of my page, split
into red rule and blue lines. they have grown stale,
yellowed, the edges curling into itself from the forceful
hold of time, but it is shelter enough for me for these
few moments, for the first few seconds of my birth.

eventually, when She beckons me forward, and
i leave my stationery shell of comfort, tendrils
of warmth releasing their grasp on my skin, i feel
unbearably *real*. i can feel the imperfect pounding of
my heart in the bone of my head, can almost taste the
iron of the ink trickling inside my veins. my flesh
feels scrubbed open, pink and red with vigour. the
price of life is death, after all.

yet She looks at me with trained disdain, the menacing
hold of Her pen angled at me accusingly. *What have
you got to show for yourself? What makes you different,
unique – what about you changes something in me?*

and i look up at her, tremblingly bare, the frost of
judgment icing over my skin. She is my creator,
my being, my life. She is my god, for she has my
life dripping out of the piercing point of her pen.

... /

She clicks her tongue, my eyes, my body, every
disfigured inch catalogued with the omnipotence of
her mind. *You are not good enough,* She says.
*You taste of the sweetness of dewdrops. But you are
not enough to make my tongue throb, to be the
sinful drops of ambrosia that I desire. There is
not enough in you for me to call home.*

You do not have enough of me in you to be perfect.

and that is rejection, packaged into a polite parcel,
exchanged coolly like business details. but for me,
with Her, this is akin to the disowning of a child by
its mother. to me, this makes the pounding of my heart
come to an insignificant halt and makes the ink of my
blood freeze into cloudy red crystals inside me. my skin
turns pearly white, the suffocating colour of death,
my paper cradle is crumpled in the infinite fist of Her
hand, and i leave, becoming past tense.

....

my only revenge is that with me, i take a thin slice of her, a tiny shard of the mirror of her soul.

....

She sighs, in my aftermath. a graveyard of crumpled paper lies around her, a field of my slaughtered siblings leaking ink onto her floor.

Again, She says, taking Her pen, brandishing it dangerously over another blank sheet of paper, but then She hesitates. for a moment, there is nothing but the echo of silence, and the musk of inspiration.

Oh, She says. *I have another idea.*

the adjudicator

the ominous ticking of the clock, oh, how it ties me to this singsong, repetitive melody of existence, how i wish and beg for a world with purest, distilled silence, siphoned off into its essence, poured over my ears, a sacred ritual, bathing me in agonising bliss and blissful agony. comfort nestles into my muscles, yet the rustle of cotton and silk grates against my nerves. serendipity bleeds gradually into my irises, yet the mean whispering of the trees clamps me in a damp jail of riverbank and bush.

the aching gleam of the lightbulb, oh, how it slices through my eyes, dices my lenses into hundreds and thousands, how it decries the luminance of my unbothered thoughts with a ray of pain. oh, how i hope and dream of a world where the world is an extension of me, where it is a canvas dyed with the paint of my tears and the watercolour of my sweat, where nothing shines, glistens, nor glints, only remains as it is, all equally attention-grabbing, all still and patient. my mother's laugh crashes against the beach, but the saltwater stings my dried skin.

the pulsing stab of the chilli, oh, how it envelops
my tongue in a fury of sun and acid, coats liberally
and coolly, a guerrilla war all across the ripened
battlefield. oh, how i wish for a world where all food
is soft and mush, where it slips and coaxes obediently,
trustfully, where it tastes of the dregs of an afternoon nap,
unaccountable and delicious, where it is borne of the
waxy sweetness of banana and the playful tease of grain.
life slides into the roof of my mouth, but the laughter in
my ears and the burning in the voices rouse a flame in me.

i fade, silently, still, sweet. the world revolves
around and around, loud and bright and spicy and
unforgiving, and me, i find the worst in the most
serene, discover the flaws in the most flawless.
everything outside of my thoughts is beautiful,
is magnificent and freeing, but i learn to find the
worst. oh, how i wish for a world where comfort
is simple, where serendipity is peaceful, where
laughter is joyous and bubbling. how i wish for
a mind where all good things remain good.

sempiternal

the stench of dried blood and morose flowers,
nauseating in nostrils, breeding mushroom spores
and mould in the winds, polluting the rivers with
necrosis and death –
the second before the end, before the gristly death
of time, a soul made ready for the taking, pale
and pavid, solemn silk, a whirlwind of cloud and
mist wreathed around her knees –

already, her hair bleeds into blistering white,
fingers crease into aged pockets, mouth puckers
into a desperate bloom –
but it is too late, already, and the pure ivory of
her clothes dry into faded spiderwebs, falling
at her feet as the stink of decay swallows her
whole, bones crunching –

all around her, winged things thud heavily onto
the ground, beady eyes turn into fog and cloudy mist,
worms shrivel into baked, clotted red, and the
forest smells of change –
time runs itself dizzy, exhilarated at the edge of its
end, and the world seizes in a fit of bliss and nausea,
the sun blinking and glitching at mid-noon, as death
splays all around her.

at the beginning, or the end, there is nothing and
no one. no sickening smell of decayed flesh, no
serendipitous sound of birdsong, no silk or threadbare
cotton, yet she still stands –
beyond death, beyond life, beyond beauty and beyond
monstrosity, a being without life, a skeleton without
death, and it smells of nothing but the stars and the gods,
unkillable, unliveable –

a life beyond death is a life beyond anything, the life
of the mushrooms writhing up from the nether, the
infinite light of the sodden milky way, something
uglier than beauty –

so, when the planet breathes its final breath, and time
meets its merciful demise, among the deathless and
among the lifeless, there she shall stand: a soul made
ready for the taking, pale, pavid, and sempiternal.

open eyes at night

i wake when i go to sleep – my eyes
open in the fogginess of the lack of light,
and they blink until i see the monochrome
shades of paused light seeping through the
cracks, open to the disc of the moon, carved
into the inky black

i wake, and see with my innermost eye, the
shuddering truth i failed to see in the brisk,
harsh sunlight the unreality of reality. i sense
the individual threads sewn into my duvet,
and think of the years in which the material
will shift into felt threadbare nothingness, and
i may not be there to witness it.

the night takes hold of me, wraps around my
arms with the stiffness of silk, and keeps me
hostage in the glaring truth of it all; of the
thrumming in my veins, of the blood pumping
in my fingers – all of it becomes clear as
transparent mist over elegant pine trees.
the air has a freshness to its ever-present stale
nature, biting the insides of my nostrils, flaring
like watercolours over soggy chalked paper.
my words flow like weeds in the barren earth, dark

and twisted and gloomy painting images that
were too blurry to see with the sunlight shining
over desktops and irises, but the moon reflects it
all, pale and milky, and the words float like soup
on the satin blankness of my mind, my inner pupils
like white dinner plates, as they absorb the colour
of words in the night, to go yet again to receive
a good day's rest.

whales and rose petals (in your dreams)

it goes like this: a scene struck directly from the filaments of fever, from the nonsensical ideas and fashioning a perfectly imperfect dream, transcribed directly from the mind of a friend:

pale puffs of watery cloud, frothy and bubbling like a witch's cursed cauldron flow like cotton candy ambrosia

the sky is dappled with silver streaks of glittery madness, layered haphazardly on a baby blue canvas, softer than the fingers of a newborn baby,

as the stars sneak freely across the day-trodden mint-green, soulless shadows skip on the riverbank, hopping about like careless children –

rose petals litter the neat lands
with a romantic fervour, scattered
carefully in heaps of gentle
piles, the rose scent maturing
in the air like rainy days spent
in a lonely state –

the whales take no notice of what
lies near, bounding through the
bubbling waves in intrinsic,
swan-like grace – their humps
are littered with whispered
words and treasured secrets,
and their eyes are never open,
nor are they ever really closed.

this is the land of half-swivelled
dreams, where everything is
expected in a way nothing ever
has or will be – a picture-perfect
land that has never been set
foot upon, filled with rose petals
that will never be sensed – but
tonight, i shall pick some, and
scatter them amongst your dreams.

the antonym

many stories are told with the absence of words.
there, up with the stars, with the infinite silence,
is the sky – nothingness pinned to hearts, home to
the ultimate antonymic Something. look above,
and see the throat of the celestial creature we
breathe in the bile of, share the fronds of
time with. see, look at how it glows, christened as
space, home to none of it.

fire – our first foray into creation, into godliness –
the spit of destruction, of ashen dirt and dust; the
fumes of rebirth, the smoke of life and new leaves.
an entity so entitled that we feel it within us,
sweat and vapour, weariness. think of cold –
a feeling born of longing for flame's touch.
witness how uncaring a cold winter
night is in comparison.

look at the corners of her eyes. crow's feet, no
stranger to the sun. you think she has not suffered,
because her laugh swells like fresh yolk? you think
she knows nothing of pain, of rain, because of
how quickly she welcomes the bright blue
of midday? look again. see the dark that lives
beneath her eyes, the white, the grey, that
glimmers in her hair.

see how things grow. see how love gets in all of the
gaps, makes it muddy and damp, moulds it into a glob
of susceptibility and wisdom. you see what is there,
not what wasn't. the sky is black, yes, but that's
because the stars were white and blue and explosion
orange! fire burns, scars, yes, but look at how
the blankets lay limp without it, how your body
yearns when snow falls. look at her smile,
but look at the places where it doesn't quite
fill, where the photo albums and incense are.

all or nothing

the wind paints the windows a dusty shade, colours
the song of the world in tones of uneasiness. whispers
gather beneath the air, hiding under the dull ringing of
silence. no use for words, not anymore. lately, life
has been undertones, in some way, pushed aside
for the drone and buzz of work, of desire. the ocean,
outside, borders the lights of the city. a shape without
shape, ominous in its absence.

there seems to be an awful lot of things missing, now.
before, there used to be things you could write about,
things to love. the sun still rises now but it feels as
if it's not worth much writing about it anymore.
what is life, even? an arrangement of isolated incidents,
each multiplied by the other in an exponential
series until the very last incident, of which
nothing comes after.

what use is there in loving the sun, loving the moon,
when love is just an incident? things die, things live,
things rise and fall, but the self goes on anyway,
with or without love. what use is something impermanent,
when all things are impermanent? what is the use
of words, when a word is just an incident, an
insignificant fraction of an impermanent thing?

what use is it when the windows change colour?
what use is it when the air hides sound? why
should words exist, when the windows shall
one day be dust, and sound shall one day be
silence? what meaning will they offer me, when
i am impermanent, am changeable, am an incident
of a finite many?

why should a word define me, when neither
exists forever? why should i be known for windows
and greys when one day, there will be no one to
know any of them? a word is a moment, one
that can pass, can die. words have no meaning
in the grand scheme of the universe.

but now i watch, always through words. the
window is foggy, and the ocean is formless,
and the sound is beneath the air.

one day, they shall
all be gone. for now, i am here to watch.

what never leaves

one day, death shall come
creeping in through broad
daylight, in the bold, harsh
shadows painted viciously
by the sun's watchful iris

death shall stay in the form
of bland cardboard boxes,
folded neatly and orderly; they
shall host your physical life,
all you produced in the
material realm, the only real
remnant of your existence –

death shall watch through
the keyholes of your house
as the clockworks of life
keep creaking on without
you – your loved ones will
move on, because it is in
human nature to triumph
through adversity –

all will be
all right, an impossible
equation in which you have
no value in – death comes,
and stays and watches, but
never leaves – never stops

lingering in sad smoke
and old song records, never
gives you the privilege of
forgetting – which might be
the best thing about death:

it is sadness, depression, nostalgia –
but it is real – painfully, stubbornly
real – one-day death shall come, but
you will never have the pleasure
of having it leave.

stolen

the water laps at her legs, taunting her with its lulling rhythm. it freezes the blood in her body, then boils it all up again in a single, devastating breath, and the sea-shaped sand laughs at her from its place on her clothes. the wind burns her skin more than usual, shrieking in her ears with an unbearable fury.

such is the price of grief: the screams are louder when there is no one else to hear them.

the ocean has something of hers. something that belonged to her, whom she loved in the way the horizon opens up its arms to the sun at the end of a gruelling day. this water, salt and sand, has stolen her sun, the light in her eyes and the glimmer of the waves – everything that she loved in this world, taken from her in the passing of a wave, in a single stolen breath.

such is the price of grief: what happens seems so simple for how many worlds it ends.

apparently, his ashes will find their way back
here, the dust of his bones taking the place
of the last breath he ever took in this wretched
sea. for her, it was shock, then anger, then
rage and fury … and now she searches for
acceptance in the red heart of the sunset.
how foolish had her darling sun been, to
have fallen in love with this cruel behemoth
they called the sea, to have been enamoured by
the way his body shimmered in its waves, to
have been seduced by its deep, unreachable
depths.

such is the price of grief: no matter how much
she loved him, it wasn't enough. he still left.

but she knew she loved him, knew he loved
her too. it was enough, it was more than enough,
and that was the problem, wasn't it? she loved
him enough for him to know that she was willing
to grieve for him. she knew from the beginning –
but it still hurts, oh, how it hurts, that he went
and left her,to watch this ruined horizon without
him, to look at this gaping sea and see death.

such is the price of grief: it wasn't her fault. it wasn't
anyone's fault (~~but she blames the sea~~),
it still happened.

                                                       … /

and so she sits here, without a lover, a crashing
monster of foam and bubbles inside her where
there should have been light and salt-dusted smiles
instead. he was stolen from her, and she is left
with the thief sipping the hollowness of her legs.
there was an exchange, somewhere where she
blinked and missed it, and the next morning she
woke to the apocalypse.

none of it was fair, none of it *is* fair –
and such is the price of grief.

about the author

Sanuli Karunaratne is a 15-year-old Sri Lankan Australian writer. She won the Junior Secondary section in the prestigious Dorothea Mackellar Poetry competition in 2024 for her poem 'I Have an Idea', and was awarded the Walter Welburn Prize for the best poem by a Country Junior Student in the Spring Poetry Competition for her poem 'whales and rose petals (in your dreams)'. She also received second and third place in the Insight Creative Writing Competition in 2024 and 2023, respectively, for her poems 'summer' and 'dance of the day'. She was one of eight shortlisted writers in the Dymocks 'Beyond Words' Creative Writing Competition and was also longlisted for the same competition in 2023. She also received an Honourable Mention in the 2023 What Matters writing competition in Tasmania. Having migrated from Sri Lanka six years ago, she currently resides in Burnie, Tasmania, with her family, and enjoys reading, drawing, and thinking about doing things but never quite getting around to them.

www.ingramcontent.com/pod-product-compliance
Lightning Source LLC
Chambersburg PA
CBHW061212070526
44583CB00025B/3217